The Red-Funnelled Boat

Peter Armstrong was born in Blaydon on Tyne in 1957. He trained as a psychiatric nurse, and more recently has worked as a cognitive therapist in Newcastle. His poems were included in *Ten North East Poets* in 1980 and his first collection, *Risings*, was published in 1989. He received an Eric Gregory Award in 1981. He lives in Northumberland with his wife and two children.

Peter Armstrong

The Red-Funnelled Boat

PICADOR

First published 1998 by Picador

an imprint of Macmillan Publishers Ltd
25 Eccleston Place, London SW1W 9NF
and Basingstoke

Associated companies throughout the world

ISBN 0 330 36914 8

9 8 7 6 5 4 3 2 1

A CIP catalogue record for this book is available from
the British Library.

Phototypeset by Intype London Ltd
Printed and bound in Great Britain by
Mackays of Chatham plc, Chatham, Kent

for Aelred Stubbs, CR

Contents

ACKNOWLEDGEMENTS

Some of the following poems have appeared in:

Agonie (Germany); *Bête Noire*; *The Echo Room*;
High on the Walls (Morden Tower/Bloodaxe Books);
Poetry Review; *The Printer's Devil*; *The Rialto*;
Skoob Review; *Other Poetry*.

The Red-Funnelled Boat

Comrades, since it's evident
that the voices teasing us at nightfall
with their inklings of another island
where Jerusalem might be builded,
are at best of shady origin,
and more likely beg the question
of the demon in the synapse,

let's go line up at the jetty
for the red-funnelled boat to take us
by black-watered sea-lochs
to its approximate asylum
– *aliéné, égalité, fraternité*
inscribed on the gateposts
and the inside of the inmates' foreheads –

where we might hope to be permitted,
under the benevolent dictatorship
of the monthly needle,
to establish our republic
of tweeds and decorum:
one last collective indulgence
in the dreams of the mind politic.

Between the ashlar ward-blocks
and the rusticated boundary,
the light will be democratic
on the backs of garden details
and the chronically second-sighted,
the electrodes reserved only
for those weeping over their Isaiah.

Tell those who come after
how we boarded in one body,
feeling, but not flinching at
the bow's one long incision
down the firth's dark mirror:
the red stump of its funnel lifted
as high as it was ploughing under.

Figures Beneath the Tree of Healing

(An allegory)

However long those seeds, those ash-keys or whatever,
have been twisting down the shadows beneath the lowest
branches,
these chiaroscuro veterans have neither brushed them from their
jackets
nor mentioned how they gather like a dandruff on their
shoulders;
how they drop into the beakers of what must be small beer
for all they hint at rum and could be whispering of laudanum.

The brims of their hats have grown improbably wide; their
faces,
apart from one white shock of eye, have lost themselves, or
tried to,
in scarfs and frozen postures. Meanwhile the lightning goes
unnoticed,
scratching its bright signature above that sleeping town there
we'll assume is dreaming deluge, regicides and so on;
though apparently the waterways have quietly frozen over,
the apprentices tarred-and-feathered this year's would-be-
dominies
(or whatever is the custom); and later at the guildhall
the burghers and the mercenaries will have signed another
contract
florid with allusions to the coming peaceful decade.
The millennium as far off or immanent as ever,
why now they turn a shoulder on the shell of night behind
them?
– what we need here is a label.

———

What we need here is a label
that would tell us, being simple, the agony and the obvious:
how the big-arsed friar doubles the bishop of wherever
and the gibbeted skin-and-ribcage is the image of the chancellor;
how the artist is that inn-keeper and his mistress is the prostitute
lounging at the church door (meaning something in particular);
dates, precursors, studio; the tell-tales and trade secrets
that the knowing go on knowing in apartments over galleries
with their walls of minor masters, the anglepoise-illumined
manuscripts and monograms within its midnight circle,
where accents grown improbable as the bow-tie and the
                                                waistcoat
own wisdom's every syllable.
                        Or how can we endure
that rider on the highway; there, exchanging horses
at the inn beside the windmill, the stable-cobbles steaming;
that wave, top left, encroaching on the dyke the moon is edging;
those herds or flocks or people strung across the pastures
or the marshes, or the outside shadow might prefigure?

Let five o'clock deliver the parquet from its echoes,
and the blinds across the rooflights be drawn back to uncover
a night sky overarching these essays in night-colours:
the seeds will go on falling without falling any lower;
the faces stare, or not stare, at the absent viewer;
and whether everything is ending or nothing much is
                                                happening,
the dust day redistributes relaxes into tenure.

Perhaps the dyke is giving and the hoards are creeping nearer
to everything that's civil, the one unlifted drawbridge

unguarded in the moonlight, the guard draped round his lover;
or perhaps the dust will gather in drifts that each night deepens
while the city night outside goes on repeating itself forever.
These, from their slight eminence, this somewhere safe or clever,
may have looked and looked away before the whole shebang is

over

or have come to greet the Kingdom, or are following their

orders,

or are carrying on regardless; and how would we discover?

Sunderland Nights

(for Maurice Pierce, on hearing of his ordination)

Brother,
        word has come, a grey decade after
our questionable mysteries, that you have put on black.
Pray for us, who, rat-arsed in high-ceilinged bars
dribbled metaphysics into our beer
and wanted women.
        Remember the stations we kept,
neon or the moon glancing off a wet road,
an east wind harassing
the sad provincial streets. God and alcohol:

I see you hunched over your smoke
and drink: "Tonight I knelt in my room
and repented of my sins"; and me
yelling back across the swamped formica table
my crack-brained marriages of Paul and Sartre.

But let that be,
for now you come to mind I see us
stumbling to some outlying town,
aimless circling speech having petered into silence,
a quick-moving stranger gaining ground behind us.

An Englishman in Glasgow

(for Steph and Alistair Wilson)

Let the rain be padding its fingers
    on the soft drum of a car
and the high-built crescents stretch
    into a temperate Bohemian dusk,
a lax, acceptant exegesis
    of the parable of Friday night.

I could go on circling that maze
    of greenery and presbyterian frontages,
the Kremlins and the Gormenghasts
    dreamed into a municipal park,
the reductionist bars stood preaching
    their one true work-ethic of drink,

could smuggle back across the border
    this weather-smudged contraband,
have the dormitory villagers
    stripping back their oak-beamed lounges
to the concrete ceiling,
    to the strip-lit nub of things,
hunched above their halfs and chasers,
    dreaming accordions, republics.

In Transit

Whether these beside me are the unbaptized
shuffling without blame or hope
from one arse-end of a city to another,
or this is the Church Suffering
as my blue-rinsed catechists never painted it,
there remains the puzzle of these passing:
sleeping faces slabbed against their windows
en route for places distant as fabulous.

And these mornings that have found us
crashed out over rucksacks and moulded chairs
may have stirred in some a lust
or virtue that would have them follow
last night's half-lit woman's face
to beatitude or some midland town,
but we all slink back at nightfall
to our bored high-fives and this companionable gloom

to wait for ticket-desks to open
and tomorrow's tabloid back-page colour.
And, anyhow, when the sun picks out
a slow ascending genie of cigarette-smoke
and talk defers to a perfect unhoping silence,
who wouldn't almost love this place,
these afternoons stretched
between diesel-fumes and fast food,

or, watching as the last bus goes
half-empty down the cracked concrete forecourt,
rest discontent, savouring this dusk,
the first street-lights and the last day-sky
the blue and gold of paradise, or of Brazil.

Quo Vadis?

On coming on a postcard from Paul Theroux in North Tyneside

i

And so there is that brotherhood,
that close-on-silent order
mumbling their office in the dark of a platform buffet,
sending back their punched stubs
from grass-grown mythic termini,
tinted postcards of the lost funicular,
unimaginable gauges.

ii

Halfway through the next millennium
whatever medium will have blessed its children with a *noir*
will already have assumed these ill-lit offices,
this slick patois pretending amorality,
the dialects half binding
DA's to the dicks;
                and so to the Hornby relics,
the dog-eared three-months' timetable
no-one ever ran; summit gradients;
the slide-rules of the blessed Nigel Gresley:
all the sacred apparatus revenants
and thugs would do you for.

You walk in on the friendly chat,
the one bulb in the ceiling dancing
so the blood on his lapel stands out as black;
'Lahore,' they say, 'You must have memories of Lahore.'

iii

You'll find him reading in the carriage corner
unencumbered by the stats or cans of Tennants
tertiaries have cultivated;
practicing a phrase against that passing town,
Europe figured in the one benighted peasant
stooping in the corner of a field.

Don't disturb him;
that the clacking web should be remembered,
Gregorian announcements under great arched roofs,
DMUs on valley-lines of willowherb,
that we should wake to find
the night train riding over a river plain, the corridor still empty,
water mirroring a blue dawn
and sliding to a different sea.

The Seeds of Doom

Starring Jon Pertwee

As usual the end is nigh:
the yokels and disposables
have gone with scream and bulging eye
to ends far-fetched as horrible,
not knowing that the end was nigh.

Inevitably, the scheme misfired
with cataclysmic consequence;
the project everyone admired
has turned out with a difference,
and, anyway, the Prof was hired

or duped by some black-suited ghoul
with global rule in either eye,
who, now he sees the outcome whole,
suspects the end might just be nigh,
and looking deep within his soul

concludes that wisdom counsels *Get
out of here while you can fly*
and leaves the sludge-beleaguered set,
the end of which is surely nigh,
to Pluck and Goodness, dropped in it

by means less clear than fortunate,
to cast an undespairing eye
on veg. acquiring appetite
and powers-that-be stood gormless by
the end of their, or any, state.

The women scream and show their legs;
tendrils slither at the door.
Et, Voila! While the heavy begs
for mercy at the drooling maw,
Maestro conjures from the dregs

of probability and chance
denouements played *ff*; and with
a flourish of deliverance
whips off the cloth (a.k.a. *Death*)
and All is Well. We breathe. He grins.

The theme tune's phrases rise and die;
the minutes re-assume their tack:
a weekend that goes mooching by,
the weekdays that keep mooching back,
while all our yesterdays descry

an autobiographic slack.
The end is nigh or never nigh;
the credits roll across the black.

A Litany in Honour of St David

i

Children, know that this is not the real world   **Juantorena**
and that these priests and victims
exultant or collapsing at the finish   **Juantorena**
must hand the baton to their unlovely doppelgängers
milling in the shadows of the tunnel,   **And who cares who's third?**
must go back to their marriages and flats,   **Juantorena**
slack pecs troubling the mirror, and the neighbour
playing his steel drum at midnight.   **Juantorena, off the final bend**

ii

Or consider this wet Saturday,
the wind making its announcements
in the caverns and the corrugations
of the oxidizing roof:
one-nil down and on the cusp of relegation,
our failing saviours breathless on the wing,
groundsmen and wrecked veterans
dream into May their every lost Wembley.
Down among the trampled programmes
go career details, second team appearances.

According to the place and season,
here the people say   **Asa Hartford**

iii

Children, there will come a time
the grey screen fuzzes over the doings of the perfect,
and the ubiquitous East German
has come up to the shoulder of all that's fine and noble.
Whose voice would not be breaking
or whose syntax, if the destined, for this once,
have not turned their ankle on the kerbstone
or suffered that fluke rebound off the wall?

Asa Hartford   **Such a whole-hearted player**
Juantorena   **Opens his legs and shows his class**

From the Virtual Terraces

It will be late some rainy afternoon
that you will push through level four
to find the manic spiders, and the concert grands
with incisors where the white notes were,
have given on a smudgy town,
smoke or low cloud obscuring your score;
where the scuttling aliens went,
the filing masses and their grave roar.
The edges of the screen grow vague;
your finger hesitates on *fire*.

It will be 4pm some January Saturday,
the crowd stood macked and capped beneath
drizzle freezing down the touchline shadows,
we will access the Third Division North,
en route, in theory, for the Stadium of Light,
the ball describing arcs around captain's feet,
Roy, presumably, or his seven-figure son
dribbling for the dark beneath the terrace roof,
the incidental net preparing to bulge
and GOAL! appear and disappear in gold
across the instant replay. Your fingers
chafe and numb; you can feel the graphic weather
in a front from Accrington
to the heaven of slick-haired wingers,
the caser's lacing printed into your brow.

It will be dark by the time we exit
whatever programme left us here,
beaten on away goals in Reykjavik
or Sofia. The blue fuzz on the idle screen
will light us from our flickering bedrooms
where later we will turn in pyrexial sleep,
dreaming ourselves through the alleys and arcades
of a virtual Madrid, lost at five to three,
picked at last to face Real.

We Apologize for this Interruption to Our Programmes

And whether it's the library still
of Wembley, or some other sacred patch
the rain or cracking signal has abolished,

for instance Acker Bilk will usher us
across whatever empty shore we've washed up on,
cradling our four-packs and our terrace memory

against the cold thing coming:
that square of black between
The Queen and morning TV big-smile *HI!*'s.

Oh, this is the sky above the floodlights, people;
this is the limbo where the programmes go
to join the days that Gregory robbed the peasants of.

What's to do, then, lumbar-wrecking on the couch,
discovering the gas fire hissing by you,
the freezer humming to itself,

but mumble our responsaries of
Law and Charlton;
Finney, Blanchflower, Charles

and let sleep fondle us away
down tunnels and Home changing-rooms
of steam and bawdy full-backs;

the bootrooms or the boardrooms
to which we've almost gained admittance
when whatever wakes us, wakes us.

And whether it's the manager,
all cufflinks and stigmata,
or some or other night-slot host

staving off the final
grey snow of the dead screen,
the particular chill of upstairs,

what's to say but Good Night
to your landing window double;
mutter a *Nunc Dimittis*

for night-watchmen
turnstile-keepers,
lost wives.

The Demon in the Synapse

'It is well enough established. . . . that there is no criterion for telling our dreams from waking life and real sensation; and therefore the phantasms we get when we are awake and have sensation are not accidents that inhere in external objects, and are no proof that such external objects exist at all. So, if we are to follow our senses without further reasoning, we shall do well to doubt whether anything exists.'

Thomas Hobbes' 'First Objection' to Descartes

'The most intimate thoughts, feelings and acts are often felt to be known to and shared by others, and explanatory delusions may develop, to the effect that natural or supernatural forces are at work'

The ICD10 Classification of Mental and Behavioural Disorders, World Health Organization, Geneva 1992: Clinical descriptions and diagnostic guidelines; Paranoid Schizophrenia

'In severe cases, grandiose or religious delusions of identity or role may be prominent, and flight of ideas and pressure of speech may result in the individual becoming incomprehensible'

Ibid; Mania with psychotic symptoms

'**Catatonia** (κατα, according to; τονος, bracing) . . . in which the patient remains in the same position, behaving very much like a statue'

Black's Medical Dictionary, tenth edition 1931

'**Mood-Congruent Psychotic Features:** Delusions or hallucinations whose content is entirely consistent with the typical depressive themes of personal inadequacy, guilt, nihilism, or deserved punishment'

'Criteria for Severity/Psychotic/Remission specifiers . . . Major Depressive Disorder' From DSM-IV; American Psychiatric Association 1994

The ... graphs below depict prototypical courses:

C. Recurrent, with full interepisode recovery, superimposed in Disthymic Disorder (also code 300.4)

D. Recurrent, without full interepisode recovery, superimposed on Disthymic Disorder (also code 300.4)

Ibid; Longitudinal course specifiers

'**MANIA** (μανια, fury) is a form of mental disorder characterized by great excitement (*See* INSANITY)'
Black's Medical Dictionary

John Omer

From the empty flat above her empty flat
across the yellow-lit city John Omer is calling tonight.

The lights swim deep in the black mirror of the roads
and the wind is playing Ocean to the sandstone bluffs of the
asylum walls

but there is a son lies face-up under the wincing mortuary
lights,
and soon the children will be playing ball with his putty-faced
head:

so says John; so she goes,
head-scarf ravelling and unravelling like a broken spinnaker
about her,

and would be lost among the night's sea-voices
but for that one voice, murmuring from its dark hub,

matter-of-fact and monotone: who would doubt John's word
having heard it? Who wouldn't cast a steady, disbelieving eye

on these young men ushering her away,
their little cricket's voices chirruping in silly unison?

Or smile behind the red-shaved nape of PC Z,
the squad-car pitching up the drive and John having wheedled
in along the dial?

Listen down the corridors: every night the footsteps
where a corner turns, and no one there when you turn it;

someone sniggering, or something like it,
down the fresh-painted walls of silk magnolia.

From Our Man in Mania

RADIO PIECES

1:

of course, we're having trouble with the line:
since the factions have gone hand-to-hand
along the burning corridors that span
being the voice that speaks for the land
and main attraction at next Wednesday's
Firing Squad Tonight, we're never sure
if out there catches what in here says
or what version; or what, if you should hear

you'd make of all these bits of dialect,
the none- and near-sense crossing waves mid-air,
what with the tracers and the alphabet
and the codes etc. gone haywire.

I'm not sure if you're hearing me just now
but one last point . . . (AND WE'LL BE BACK ON
                                    THE HOUR . . .)

2:

. . . another rifle-volley, Lorimer;
this floor or the next one up. And the wings
are growing harder to mark tight than were
your masters of the dribble; but these things
don't elegance the front page like the back
and the smoke like tape unravelling is
blowing down the boulevards of black;
what's going on behind's all guesses.

The tiny people huddle in their basements
and we few of the microphones grow vast,
immunized against whatever's zipping past
the ducking soundman's lug. At nights our tents
are shrines to this year's cargo-cult, The News;
the mayor's wife sells herself with scrapes and bows.

COLUMN INCHES

2nd of June: again the dark-faced crowds
have been in spate along the boulevards.
Between the tenements and favelas,
surrounding the rococo palace
of the cardinal, they have flooded
all day through their bayou of alleyways.
Last night another hill-storm paraded
its fire-power overhead; today's
weather is all politics.

          And with dark,
whispers of resignation have become
this chant we hear: a dark, triumphal hymn
to the piazzas' blood-beat. Sirens, arc-lights
scything the night sky are pronouncing
Eden commenced. Even the guards are
                    singing . . .

FROM THE DIARY

It was that night-speech on the balcony
when I'd squeezed on like some side-kick of the Pope
& heard & saw the locals play the Kop
beneath their new Dalglish
(or name your favourite man in red
or what colour and what end you'd want)
thumping out *Eh Pyro! Pyro Eh!*
their arms upstretched and all
that rhythmic latin stuff

it dawned how clever we'd all been, and how
El Lipido out there
busting from his uniform
and rumoured corset knew sod all.
I kept my counsel and eyed up his wife,
sneaked a wave to Mario
(or Georgio or Karl)
conducting the ovations three rows back
and bit my grin.

ON THE EVE OF THE TRIUMPHAL ENTRY

Entering the shack, of course the walls lit up; the woman's face
reshaped itself before me like a holy thing.
It was like that every hovel after each: treading
with the silences of midnight on our soles, we'd trace

the Glorious Mysteries from humble plot to plot.
The children snuffled in their cradles
and the moon came up. Idols
on their corner altars shuffled from the light,

knowing what they knew. And even when the dawn
came picking out the shadows in their ruts
and the smokes of those thin breakfasts
rose against the glass-faced towers in the sun

there was a knowing quiet down the streets:
the men, you'd say, would hardly bow,
but let them have their pride for now;
the women offered spices at my feet.

A LETTER TO THE EDITOR

And all these months I've written and you've laid
my copy at the bottom of the page
between the livestock prices and the vague
disseminations of the Vatican brigade;
If I'd still failed to take the hint by now,
that hand across the mouth, this room, these men
who hold the Luger to my temple, show
explicitly what you were hinting then.

I say this in a measured voice tonight;
(they chained my ankles to the bottom of
the desk you haven't paid for yet). O, love
I fear the mortars less than my own fright;
the end less than your absence. I'd not guessed
how much of this was mine; how I'd been blessed.

Across the Great Depression

... so that left only me,
and the black dog picked up
in what passes for a town
down along the minus contours,
the rivers that go running
with their backs to the sea.

I forget how long along
the mad paving of that dead floor
before the dog-talk sifted into sense:
waking as it licked the green out
from the corner of my eye, the fissures
where my lips forgot to meet,
I'd hear it gravel – *sotto voce*,
like the natives said their prayers –
Further out and further down!
over and again and spitting to the left,
or chanting his lugubrious Baedeker:
You must see the empty quarter yet,
the sickle-moons of sand that wait
to swallow whole your every step
(further out and further down!). We must
map the salt road's dry extremes,
the abandoned philadelphias
of the upturned foothills
 – circling me widdershins all the while
and never once his sunk eye
shifting from the one last skin of water
slapping at my shoulder.
The mountains jogged

with my every step
and kept their distance.

Even when the flora
surfaced from whatever
dug-out it had minded
there among the moon-rock
and the shadows of the scarp-face,
there he was, all nuzzle
in the hollow of my ear
muttering *the skin was but a crust* –
one step hurried over-quick
and the whole caboodle
would go trapdoor underfoot.
It was somewhere in between
the first mud of the wadi
and what must have been the monastery
(I forget the days, the waking
to each dumb beneficent face)
one or other of us lost the knack
of the speaking or the hearing
and he'd skulk off at a stone's throw
barking like a foreigner
or an Englishman at one.
I won't bore you with the sand-worms
and the snakes of salt,
that mirage of the twenty-fifth
 – when they found me at the rail-head
beating off the camels
from a puddle in the gutter,
the dog lay on its belly
and welded shut his jaws against

the indulgences of water.
These mornings when I open
my light-infested curtains
he'll be skin and skull below me
in the rhododendron's shadows,
the happy rats obese
from the scraps he never takes.

Letters from Catatonia

i

The last town's dry wood
and a loose pane banging in the wind,
black-scarfed women glimpsed
as a door smacked shut;
and the birds mourning
across that sad-grassed plateau,
and the streamless gully
where the road gave out:

to step out from behind the wheel then
was to slough a skin,
to feel the air as a needle in the wound
and love its aseptic discipline,
its reductions of the flesh;
these bones picked clean . . .

ii

Or try to say
the way those last thin dribbles fingered
from the stone onto the clay
and fizzed the way my spittle did:
Dry, you might conclude, is Beauty,
but so what? and anyway
what it is is dry.

iii

The lizards come and say their prayers;
the trees yield up a company
of Spanish Saviours.

Now lift that beaker
to the yellow peelings you could paint as lips.
Mould yourselves another attitude of wax.

Gulls that must be wheeling out from land;
a scratch of river-bed the rain forgot;
this wind that dreams the snakes out of the sand.

The Psychologist's Companion

i

How long has she suspected him,
stumbling among her acolytes
all tweed and inky fingers,
great knit brow and bitten pen; the first
to give his blessing to the anglepoise,
the electricity, whatever gear would map
the sad enclosures of his cranium.
She finds him mumbling above her
when she looks up from the screen.
He knows her every reference off by heart.

ii

There is a twilight where the voices come:
she has heard herself be weighed and be found
wanting to their scrutiny. By turns
sleep and waking muscle at
their debatable lands and borders.
By turns she pays protection
to the one or to the other.

iii

Even hunkered in her bedroom corner
there were sheaves and sheaves
unloading from his grip, a fortnight's muck
ingrained into the thickness
of his specs. She knows he knows
she knows he knows. *Results*, he says,
wiping off the spittle from his chin,
you always wanted more results.

Dirty Halva

After their slow processions
down the aisles of chillies, green bananas,
the open sacks of couscous and Basmati,
one has touched the brow of his Homburg,
the other folded and refolded Monday's Times,
and, sliding back the glass door of the fridge, has muttered
'but this Halva's looking dirty, wouldn't you say?'
He prods the one fat slab of beige and leaves
with that familiar click of his heels,
the miasma of cologne and leather, Garam Masala.

Later, where the wind off the river
would be blowing gulls, like pages of a broadsheet
(and vice versa) downstream past the disused quays,
the rattling hollow railway sheds, it might happen
that film would be passed from one numb pair of hands
to another; and then the long wait,
dressed too well for the hire car, no one mentioning
the face-down figure on the cobbles, his ruined suit.
And whether that's the case, or that they go
certain yards apart across the thin-grassed park
where the ghosts of cottagers unravel from the fog,
nights remain a room where a flattened slab of light
swivels back across the wall behind them
with every passing car, a ceiling smoke has turned
the shade of dirty halva; the zapped channels flashing
in monochrome succession, B movies, lapsed soap operas.

From an Imaginary Republic

Over all the grizzled province
weather will be happening to brick,
the bronchitic natives going
hollower and hollower in the cheek,
like you've seen them, walking too quick
in drizzling library footage;

and the light that's collapsing
at the back of crees and prefabs
will be found to have died
where the city gives the ghost up
in the brick-rubble back-lane
we all grew up in

and were always nearly leaving,
rehearsing one last glance along
the yards and light-spilling doorways
before boarding for the fabled
promiscuous metropolis
where the arts and tarts were coupling

but have always found ourselves again
adrift across this outback
of the white-bricked chapels
and the closed Co-Operatives,
the flexing bed of fern
smoke reassembles on the air;

lyrical with drink
have litanied the pitfallen
and glorious relegations
on a night when the clubs
were awash with voices
and the Hammond organ's thick vibrato;

but tonight the dark and the drizzle
are whispering attrition
and a soft coast's slow erosion,
the fences rust along the border
of a northerly republic
and the crossing-gates jam open;

the one frost-bitten guard
croons softly in
a dialect that's frozen.

Retreat,
or At the Bar of the Forth Hotel

Now it's clear that the staring saved
are entrenched for the decade
while the millennium gestates
in *Plain Truth* and the Book of Daniel,
and that the city's corners
and bird-thick monuments
are the fifty-first state in waiting,

let's be reconciled to this long bar,
the spring light vetted by
an acanthus etched repeatedly
in frosted glass;
the one face opposite
staring back amiably
between the upturned spirits;

and if you should catch,
high up and half-heard
in an unattended corner,
the TV singing in its primaries
of a land of domes and diamonds,
 – men with golden arms,
the clear-skinned MVP's –

let that go as a benign fiction, Utopia
where improbably-named nose-tackles
must come good, if just once,
late some floodlit overtime,
the ball flown loose from the sack
and the end-zone open,
dyed as gold as Buddies.

Otherwise what beckons
but the west of the hoarse elect:
the last play they're calling
to pigeons and cider-heads
while the breeze is juggling
crumpled tracts and leftovers
by the doors of M&S?

The evening is agnostic,
cloudy with half-knowing.
Consider this approximate silence:
the hum of videos and unplayed bandits;
the glass seen through
with each slow raising
less and less darkly.

West

Railroaded down the grainy footages
and the dust-wrecked geometries
of a heartland,

all the legions Woody Guthrie sang
come trundling from their exodus
into a three-chord perfection,

a gauche and beautiful
rebirth on the airwaves.
Picture those motel rooms:

a smalltown band
jangling over the unread Gideons,
a nation trailing westwards

from the far side of the river.
Now let's bless those distances:
backroads laid straight

from a fenced country
into the Nirvana of prairie;
or drive out

to the dying fall
of a steel guitar,
the lonesome play of the wind,

across the dark and the wires,
Hank Williams fooling no-one with
I saw the light.

Blues

Less the voices than the rain
tapping at the window of every 78
that leaves you hang-dog and reverent
at the station or the crossroads,
witness to a denimed underclass
beautiful on ramshackle porches
and in low bars; whose untrue women,
bad pay, desertions and oppressions
get their come-uppance under
a glass-paper voice, the subversive
run of a guitar.
                    Quiet now:
over the dark a lovely sorrow drifts:
a slow freight rolls north, a child cries.
Tomorrow's millstone blurs against
another beer and a seventh chord.

Road Movies

Freedom lies beyond the Bates Motel
where the back-route towns
turn a shoulder to the wind

and a second-hand Chevy lumbers
over the hog-backed road into nowhere.
Here's the edge and here's over:

sand or snow against the windshield
and the open/closed signs
spinning on the verge.

The shades and the soundtracks,
the slick one-liners
and that poise behind the wheel:

you come this far
and then there's only style
to trade or to believe in. So,

the low sun shining
on the hubcaps' chrome
and the radio turned loud,

you'll let the silent locals
and the serial killers
shrink to bit-parts at the diner

while America drones past
trailing crumbs of neon
and its vague dream realising westwards.

The white lines roll beneath you
and your hair blows back;
the radio is teasing to a V8 throb

that just across the top of the hill
Maybelline may be waiting,
a seaboard, anything.

North of Thunder Bay
or Highway 61 Reconstituted

What should wait for the pilgrim is sky
as wide as the Delta's but whiter,
hanging its big cold dome of a roof
over a landscape of thaws and conifers:
if you listen, the Harley's wrecked engine
will be idling down to a silence
and the wind will have picked up the phrasing
of any number of road songs,
laying its plaintive harmonica
on this consummate slow fade north.

A stride piano is echoing
further and further behind you
with its whore-house paraphernalia,
where outside on the veranda
the sun is stripping the paint down
and the street below is melting
under its white-walled tyres.
And, mornings at the edge of waking
to the droning of a Greyhound,
you have dreamed or half-remembered
the ghosts and the messiahs
in the corner of a box-car:
perfectionists of exile
with their first whiff of the frost.
From the queen bleeding in the gutter
to Zimmerman idle in Hibbing
that whole procession northbound

has rolled across the parallels
like so many great sleepers,
all bound for Sweet Home New Jerusalem,
its stock-yard square mile bellowing
and the wind on the face of the faithful
thick with Michigan's sherry wine.

But you have ridden over
a long unlyrical border
where the ship that never came in lies
at sad perpetual anchor:
the band is playing Dixie
except the key is minor
and the roadsigns bleach to nothing
on the far side of the water.

The roadsigns bleach to nothing
and the wires sing a cappella
of a clean and rhythmless skyline
that the highway brings no nearer.
Beyond the four-shack city
with its LAST GAS BEFORE TUNDRA!
the roadsigns bleach to nothing
or they label something final:
the little, the less, and the ice-line,
the hiss at the end of the vinyl.

Disclaimer

The events, characters and firms portrayed in this photoplay
are purely fictitious

And this is not Geography, friends:
these bluffs, these bowls of dust,
these rivers twisting in their gleaming queries

pledge no allegiance to the map. The town
where you slowed for the lights and stopped
to watch nothing happen to perfection

was pure frontage: you knew it was, knew the silence
that would fill the drug-store shelves
the moment that you breezed in off the street

and asked for liquor or the road you'd missed; as if
the check-out queue could answer for itself, as if
the man in mirror shades had never said

'This isn't language, lady;
these are lines.' How long
before you learned to idle through,

 – the smoke of bluegrass on the country stations
drifting in the wake of your open-top,
a hinterland exploding in the mirror of its chrome –

to that miles ahead: the gas-stop with its eaten walls,
the road-towns where Methuselah
would be chewing at his gums,

the truckers playing at Titanic
on a dusty switchback.
And this was never History:

the bend you couldn't hope to make,
the screes and cactus that you'd plough
sheer into the valley floor,

had been waiting in a still heat
for no one else but you; the barrier
was made to give that way, the sierra painted there.

Or was it as you caught yourself,
at least perhaps yourself,
skew-parked in the ditch between

the skyline and the badlands:
there in the wing-mirror,
riding with the land's stunt-double.

from The Labyrinth

NATIVITY

Now let the coil unwind
and you'll step weightless from its pull
like you had shed the slavver
of the umbilicus and afterbirth

like you were changing elements,
like you could call this freedom:
all the luggage overboard
and you left bobbing in the dark.

Think about the way
the river breaks its levees:
how land loses its memory;
Just so, the flesh forgets.

Only, take this ghost of thread
that winds around my finger, either
like the thread still weighs
against the moth-wing's scales

or how the lid applies its pressure
till it seems a kind of sight
against the blind eye of the mole.

A SONG OF DAEDALUS

So there's your brick gut for the augurer
your worm's mouth, wormcast hollowed-out
your river-bed gone underground
your dance-step, drain, your veins stripped out
and left for cattle to chew over,
your ravelled sleave, your knot
your inverse tree the root grew into rock
your mothergate, birthplace, drift,
your nest, cist, dig, your low road
clay, spoil, ashes, your memento.

Is this enough for you?
Should I be reading off the altitudes and dives,
the way the sun will play
across the summits of the waves
that have no architecture, any key or thread
to lose or find among their convolutions?
I'm describing my own net above it all already;
look the way this offspring ripples.
Dip your finger in the pool and pull
to make the spreading V of a wake.

EPISTEMOLOGY

Listen: a mallet's pulse, articulate bone,
Air leaning on the nerve. Between flesh
and its touched data; between tide
and tide's cargoes
                        a thread unravels in the helix,
in the blood-warm dark, and sweats light.
A thin wake of phosphor maps the labyrinth.
It wears into the lie of things; it gives and powders.

Listen how the shell trembles, the bone hammers.

EPIPHANY

In Hopi style,
its logic unassailable, I face
the vistas of the past; behind me, safe
against discovery, where the long track curls
towards a city's heart, the future lurks.
Richard Kell, *Going Forward Backwards*

And after all the while I'd pushed
the blind balls of my eyes out
into the black sponge of the air,
and waited some bright gobbet of a fact
to spark up at the tip of my nose
(it must be somewhere hereabouts;
you never get the same lost twice),
it's only now I've turned I think
the right times round for crossroads
and said the words ordained
for such-and-such occasions
and lost all clue of which way I was facing,
it's dawned (ho-ho) that here's the way it is,
O light-skulled brethren,
down among the passages
that might be here, the labyrinth
branching and re-branching out of sight
and always out however far
you crane your neck around to peer;
down among the outed liars,
the moles, frotteurs, phrenologists,

the mountebanks of touch
and sound intelligence, the never-seen
company of anachronists
who prophecy *Look back, look back*
look back, look back.

A SONG OF THE ANACHRONISTS

And here's the metronome reversing fractions for us;
here's the needle creeping outwards to the rim
scratching from its great lug of a horn
that Mind of the North, *Formby Philosophicus*
of the rain-drilled academe of valley towns,
who posits *I'm walking backwards into nothing*
to the chunter of his banjo-uke.

And Who'd deny it? Who'd have guessed
the chimneys slopping over at his back,
the great names propping up the league,
the younger intellectuals flat-capped
along the left bank of the Ribble
muttering of *ennui* and the ruin of leg spin?

Look out from the last seat of the train
and watch the film run back
wrong way off the spool;
no driver at your left,
but then you haven't yet
smacked skull-back-against

the frame that saw him go.
There. It flashes past your shoulder
into sight. Or not. Just wait.

NDE

So this must be the vestibule
where the nearly-dead have signed themselves.
(If you find me here, I'll be fingering
the wall they've catalogued with Braille);

Or that tunnel whose light crooned
Mama! from the brilliant end
with all their lives' processions
trailing absolution thick as tar. So?

Let's you and me sniff out the floor
for sloughed pelts, odours, body fluids
– any of the calling cards; just one –
as if your tourists would have queued
to step a second time
into these tepid, dark waters.

LIGHT

Or emerging, Rip-van-Lazarus from the maze of time,
my friends dressed lightly and impossibly young,
will go unnoticed by them and the novelty of light
to meet my father coming from the sea,
his hair a mess of salt and crown and kelp.
I can see us now, of uncertain age and tastes
propping up the counter of some kiosk or some bar
philosophical with drink; hunkered at the tide-line
like there was mileage in unravelling the wormcasts,
like you could read, before the next tide wipes it clean,
some oracle in these viscera of sand.

Vigils

The mesh rattles at the low of night;
the gates swing open without a sound.
Out from the precincts of the dark
the god makes its progress. Holy ground,
silence at the passing of the ark;
its acolytes move in silence through unlit

compounds. And so every dark. Ours
is a vigil with the unremarked,
ungainly growth, that continuum
of the nettle and the perfect
firestorm of willowherb; the stem
of these little hours,

the minimum offices. Should
it be asked what the yield is,
say it is the root's thread and the gestation
of the leaf. Where hazel builds
its mesh in the spoil, and ferns raise an
unkempt alliance, harvest is what cold

and the root are making of earth,
that convolvulus infiltrates the fences,
the runways thaw into green;
seed that, lodged between the stones, is
prizing open stone, unseen
as first ice in the rut, beneath

notice and surfaces: a subversive species.
After the god and the god's
entourage, wind rippling the grass,
rain glazing the yellow-lit emptied roads,
in the slow hour that greys
a low sky and pieces

the land together, we will be found
half-noticed at the eye's corner,
as the insurgent strain
of green the margins succour
is found, and found again
raising from the cleared ground

an awkward petitionary stem.
After the gate has swung shut
and the mesh sung and quietened,
being found at this one rite
of waiting, we will turn as the land
turns out of shadow, to touch the hem

of light, the root's stratagem.

Sabbath

Sun pronounces blessing on our coming here,
rolling out its yellow carpet on the suburbs,
the favelas of crees and allotments;
here, falls through opaque glass
on triumphal and obscure
plate and proof-texts, dust playing at being incense.
    The sun built this place:
we cannot raise our eyes for it.

Now, the word is a silhouette
against the blinding page (or it
has burned into the retina)
and the one who rises, blessed
with a smile artless and immaculate
has burned into his own corona.
    Who would have guessed
these brilliant extremes, these clean dichotomies?

Who hasn't craved their polar light?
– to rise, washed and without name as
Zion's gates are chocked ajar in the morning?
For look, blue-suited and benign, he has
proffered an acceptant hand that we might
give our shadows into his keeping.
    Oh, the gleaming wordy edifice
he raises, the acetylene noon;

beneath which and beneath notice goes
the sacred-hearted also-ran
to pick over the bits of Gehenna
and the desert's remnants.
Day forty, and a dry wind blows,
and you catch him from your eye's corner,
    where a brilliant devil tempts
Be one of us, brother, and believe.

The going sun touches on the faces of the saved,
as if they blushed to see their love
undress before them. The dusk, whispering
its small complicated lives, erodes
the ashlar's edge that halved
light and dark. Dismissed into the mingling,
    we will scatter down our half-lit roads
between palliative shadow, and neon barbs.

Sunderland Nights Revisited

Listen to those names again:
Enon, Elim, Hebron; strung
between the testaments and geography,
the weather coming off the sea and scratching
its grey belly on the black-spired town.

Tell the saved girls I'm backslidden now
but still adrift among those choruses,
absurd and reverent in equal measure;
and since the take-aways are shut, and kenosis
in the shape of the rain and the one slow

last car saying *hush* along the road,
is the only gift that's given us tonight,
we could walk close and quietly,
knowing the text too well to speak it
or say anything aloud,

huddled in the old coats of a faithfulness,
a promised land somewhere hereabouts
heavy with its grapevines, place-names, sea-frets.

Among the Villages

Stumbling across them among thin pastures
and the gorse-grown relics of rail
you couldn't fail to find
the air heavy with elegy,
the locals wry, but incomprehensible.

Buses going other places
yielded brief epiphanies
through the blurred arc swabbed clear
in fogged upstairs windows,
of streets besieged by weather,
terraces shored against
the ebbing tide of trade,

but you knew all that:
that whole inheritance of shales and spoils
you'd sluice clean into the work of giants.
Maybe even knew this night:
the way the light at the gable corner
lights next to nothing,
that head-scarfed woman hurrying
from history to the neighbours.

Force Eight, Barra

The house was a boulder ship
riding out a crazed westerly:
a week drinking tea
in the patched-up prow of its kitchen
listening, and then not hearing
as the wind rived at the chimney,

and we were Atlantic veterans
hunched over the crackly radio,
the exotica of coastal forecasts
driven into a salt smear
against the window.

I loved that beaten township,
the way the tarmac crumbled in among the grass;
labouring back from the Co-Op
weighed with bread and alcohol;
fetching wood from the tide-line
to hack into kindling.

And nights
when the bar of the Craigard Hotel
breathed its air of that disconsolate edge,
to be tourists, beaten up
by the indigenous wind, half an ear
to the country and western
on the stereo, the other

to the Glasgow drunk
lamenting down the houses.

Area Forecasts

Tonight the wind is off the bay
and the gulls are scavenging
along this windward shore;
the stream at the kitchen window mouths
its untranslatable
gaelic music.

Who wouldn't find religion here,
the way the cloud comes off the hills,
and bow to hear this priestly voice
navigate the wingbeats
and hushes of static: *veering north* it says,
six rising eight;

over these fingertips of Europe
chants softly *falling slowly.* And I can see
spread out like a prairie on the map
the ocean fenced into its great blue ranches,
their names a fable
daily blessing the wavebands.

Now Valentia yields
its grey acres to the sleet,
and Shannon is a plain
glinting as dull as mercury;
Hebrides, that marginal tract,
shelves out under a sky the colour of peat;

and still the voice is speaking:
across a thousand miles and more of sea
there stoop to listen
trawlermen and yachtsmen,
that cold-fingered diaspora;
at bleared windows, the shorebound

dream past their warped reflections
skies trailing hems of showers
or skies with their seamless robes
of blue. Next to nothing,
but the gannets at their diving,
stitching air to water.

Notes

The Red-Funnelled Boat

My father, who was a surgeon, had been posted to Rothesay to develop a surgical service. Medical services on the island were rudimentary apart from some exceptionally good general practitioners. My father also worked in Greenock on the mainland and other services such as Medicine and Obstetrics were provided from there which was the logical place. However this logic did not extend to Psychiatry. Psychiatric services were supplied from the Argyll and Bute Hospital which was situated at Lochgilphead. In those days community psychiatry was but a glint of an idea in some zealots' minds and so patients requiring out-patient or in-patient care had to travel to Lochgilphead. Although only 20 miles away as the seagull flies, the road journey was (and is) complicated and lengthy requiring the use of at least one small ferry and several long loops round various lochs. In view of this patients used to be transported by a MacBrayne's ferry which came into Rothesay every day at 10.30 a.m. and then travelled through the Kyles of Bute round Ardlamont Point and up Loch Fyne arriving at Lochgilphead two hours later. The MacBrayne ferry was one of many steamers who came into Rothesay at that time. MacBrayne ferries were characterized by their red funnel. This led to the colloquialism that those who were odd, strange or indeed plain nuts were 'ready for the red-funnelled boat.' Although the ferry stopped running many years ago, road transport has been improved and community psychiatry on the island now well developed, this colloquialism remains in active use.

Nicol Ferrier, Professor of Psychiatry,
University of Newcastle upon Tyne

Sunderland Nights
cf. Luke Ch. 24 v. 13.

Quo Vadis?
Nigel Gresley: designer of A4 Pacifics.
DMU: Diesel Multiple Unit.

A Litany in Honour of St David
St David: i.e. Coleman.
Juantorena: Alberto Juantorena, Cuban 400 and 800 metre runner.
Asa Hartford: Scottish midfielder of the 1970s whose transfer from Manchester City to Leeds United was blocked on discovery of a hole in the heart.

From the Virtual Terraces
Caser: i.e. a *real* (laced-up and leather) football.

Sunderland Nights Revisited
Kenosis: 'emptying' (cf. Phillipians Ch. 2v.7).

Retreat, *or* at the Bar . . .
MVP: Most Valuable Player (i.e. at Superbowl).

A Song of the Anachronists
The Tyneside Metro has blessed its passengers with seats at the very front and rear of its trains, immediately to the right of the driver's cab.

NDE
Near Death Experience.